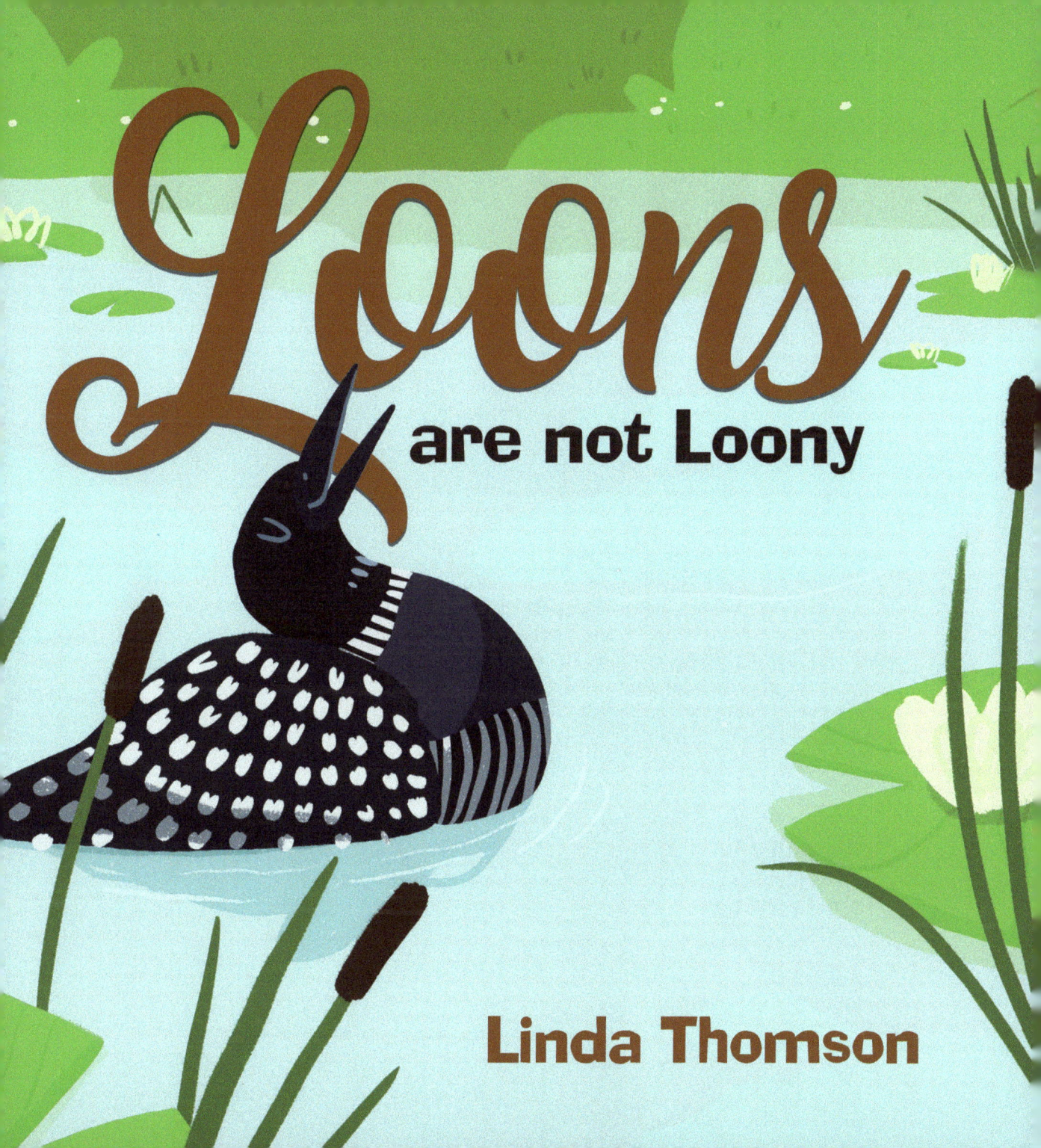

Loons are not Loony
Copyright © 2021 by Linda Thomson

All rights reserved. No part of this publication may be reproduced, distributed, or transmitted in any form or by any means, including photocopying, recording, or other electronic or mechanical methods, without the prior written permission of the author, except in the case of brief quotations embodied in critical reviews and certain other non-commercial uses permitted by copyright law.

Tellwell Talent
www.tellwell.ca

ISBN
978-0-2288-5079-3 (Paperback)

Loons are not loony.
Let me tell you why.
If they are so loony,
How do they vary
Their special cry?

Loons are not loony.
Let me tell you why.
If they are so loony,
How do they hold their breath
Without even a sigh?

Loons are not loony.
Let me tell you why.
If they are so loony,
How do they fish
Without even a try?

Loons are not loony.
Let me tell you why.
If they are so loony,
How do they carry their chicks
On their backs so high?

Loons are not loony.
Let me tell you why.
If they are so loony,
How do they form a circle
On a full-moon sky?

Loons are not loony.
Let me tell you why.
If they are so loony,
How do they adapt,
Rather than die?

Loons are not loony.
Let me tell you why.
If they are so loony,
How do they stay in the air
As they swiftly fly?

Loons are not loony.
What I think we should say
Is that loons are very clever
In a special sort of way.

Loons can be lovely
And loons can be smart.
Loons can be graceful.
But LOONY THEY'RE NOT!

www.ingramcontent.com/pod-product-compliance
Lightning Source LLC
LaVergne TN
LVHW072018060526
838200LV00060B/4701